Losing Ohio

Poems by
Gwen Hart

New Women's Voices Series, No. 9
Finishing Line Press
Cincinnati • Georgetown

Losing Ohio

This is a limited collector's edition.
Only 250 copies of this book were produced.

Copyright © 2002 by Gwen Hart
ISBN 0-9718922-5-3   ISSN 1098-8173
First Edition

All rights reserved under International and Pan-American Copyright Conventions. No part of this book may be reproduced in any manner whatsoever without written permission from the publisher, except in the case of brief quotations embodied in critical articles and reviews.

ACKNOWLEDGMENTS

"Losing Ohio," *I Have my Own Song for It*
"Friday Night in Concord, Ohio," *Touched by Eros*
"The Lights Go Out . . ." *A Christmas Anthology*
"Anniversary Poem," *Mankato Poetry Review*
"Luxuries," *Lonzie's Fried Chicken*
"Miracle," *Acorn Whistle*

Series Editor: Leah Maines
Inside Art: Leigh Dupuy Wilson
Cover Photo: Roger A. Hart

Printed in the USA.

email: FinishingBooks@aol.com

Author inquiries and orders:

Finishing Line Press
P. O. Box 1016
Cincinnati, Ohio 45201-1016
U. S. A.

Table of Contents

Twenty Years Ago	1
Miracle	2
Rondeau on Results	3
Luxuries	4
Paradise	5
The Fire Buff's Relief	6
Friday Night in Concord, Ohio	7
Losing Ohio	8
Candy Heart Sonnet	9
Rain in Boston	10
Lub-Dub	11
Mystery Hairs	12
Why I Had to Leave Town	13
Anniversary Poem	14
The Lights Go Out . . .	16
Sonnet for an Ordinary Day	17
Thief	18
Poem for the Arguing Neighbors	19
Leftovers	20
Happy Birthday	21
Woman at the Water's Edge	22
Remnants	23
The Middle of Life	24
Late Definitions	25
About the Author	27
New Women's Voices Series	28

For Roger

Twenty Years Ago

at the grocery store,
a man wheeling a cart
of frozen, packaged meat
tapped my mother
on the shoulder
to ask if he could pass.
She screamed and threw
produce up in the air,
always afraid something
was sneaking up
behind her. I was seven,
thought she was crazy,
didn't realize years
could do that.

Miracle

We dreamt
of ice-skating,
worn-out,
whispering,
on the flinty black
of the river.
We couldn't afford
skates, but carved
imaginary eights
with our boot-soles,
balled fists punched
together for warmth.
Your breath circled
up like a halo,
cloudy and brief.
The moon made
the snow on our
jackets glisten
like sequins,
and we floated,
we glided
over the water
in our heavy,
brown shoes.

Rondeau on Results

The result of amorous contortions
viewed on late-night cable television
prompted us to ask the question, "How
exactly do they do abortions?" How
Cathy's mother's face, how her expression,

changed! Her eyes closed; her mouth's distortion
twisted out an answer. "Well, some women
use a coat hanger. That much I'll allow.
The result

is sometimes death. But then, my solution
was marriage, so I've never had occasion
to know." With that, she sent us out. Our slow
progress from the house was through the snow—
bared bricks, the red startling in white's season,
the result.

Luxuries

In the fifth-grade lunchroom, I said
things like, "Hey! This cheese sandwich
is so hard, you might as well eat the plate!"

And got sent to the office for pointing out
French-toast sticks, stuck to the rafters
by their own syrup, over twenty years ago,

to date. My mother said I should be ashamed,
since my best friend Jenny was on free-lunch
tickets, and school food was the most

she ever ate. But I knew better. I gave Jenny
laughter, which at her house was scarcer
than milk and curdled faster.

Paradise

The bicycle was awful—
a no-speed piece of junk
with two mismatched tires,
a rusted pink frame,
and a cracked banana seat
smeared with huge, faded flowers,
yellow and blue,
bound by silver duct tape.
It had a basket—white with blue
and red and holes woven right in.
I was convinced Marsha Brady
wheeled it to the front curb,
leaned it against a trash can
the day she discovered boys.
I said I hated it,
but rode it anyway,
rode it every night,
pumping hard up the hills
of a street named Paradise,
thirteen
and determined to fly.

The Fire Buff's Relief

My father loves a good house fire; a gas
main break's an unexpected treat. He races
to each scene, equipped with radio
and camera, dons protective goggles so

to stand a smidgen closer to the flashing
lights, siren-calls, the water thrashing
hoses into life. This is where
he's most alive, a gentle engineer

too frail to fear the Draft, too asthmatic
for basketball, he walks a line mathematics
charts and keeps an antique fire truck
for children's charity events. What's tucked

beneath the surface rises with each thirsty
flame and second-story window's bursting.
Hate and fear, sorrow and love can choke
a man or dissipate, the same as smoke.

Friday Night in Concord, Ohio

After their teeth were brushed, their pajamas
on, their dreams drifting swiftly through the dark,
I snuck into their father's room. He was
alone, as I was, except for his work.
I had homework. Geometry could wait.
I painted my bare legs above the knees
with sticky stripes of his deodorant,
lowered my head, inhaled the rich scent—*his*,
then sank bodily into his closet.
Pantlegs brushed my breasts, shirtsleeves licked
my neck, my shoulders. My legs held apart
by his tasseled loafers, a tie, blue silk,
pulled taut against the crease beneath my skirt,
I let my body go.
                         Headlight beams lit
the room. Twin orgasms, they shook their thick
stars in my eyes, left my body stunned, slack.
His keys jangled. The lock turned with a click.
My thighs went weak. I pulled my damp hair back.
I willed myself to stand, to reach the couch.
The Angels sleep? he called. *They dream.* He slipped
the money in my glowing palm. I touched
each bill in turn, pressed each to my flushed lips.
Down the long slope of his drive, the dark street,
I breathed the leather scent of his wallet.
All around me, above me, white moths beat
themselves against the street lamps in the wet
summer air, their frayed wings flames or hearts
set aflutter by the body's secrets.

Losing Ohio

The things that stand still will, of course,
be the first to disappear--the long lip
of the curb, the squatting bushes,
the stubborn, stalled Chevy, the frozen
features of the front stoop.

You insist on running five miles a day on slippery
shit-roads with false shoulders, ditches humped
over with the snow. You run alongside traffic
until the roar of snowplows makes you jump
over, lose your legs in snow,
stand in it up to your waist.

Whole convoys will pass December this way,
flashing and dragging metal, at the end
of the road where the mailboxes hibernate,
their black, hungry mouths iced shut, bodies
shaky from the slams of road-clearers.

You sleep with your good ear muffled
in a goose-down pillow while the snow settles
over the places you know well, buckling
roofs, toppling power lines, and severing
telephone connections.

When I try to come back to you,
the plane descending not through sky,
but through the chalky white
of a snow cloud, what will be waiting?

What will I return to
if everything I've counted on
is long-buried, houses closed and hearts
steeped and shuttered in snow?

Candy Heart Sonnet

I passed the NECCO factory on my way
to work, a thousand miles away
from you, my heart a chalky
shape crushed between love's teeth. I walked
this way on purpose, read the display

window valentines. Their huge pastel
letters proclaimed TRUE LOVE, BE MINE,
NO WAY, I DO, monosyllables,
mantras I chanted, walked in time
to through the rain. Hair wet, no umbrella,

I marched right by the T station, refused
to turn around. There'll be another stop,
I told myself. HUG ME, MARRY ME, AS IF,
my fortune changing with each step.

Rain in Boston

for the third day,
and everywhere
umbrellas, overshoes,
wind like a spent breath.

The entire city
is humbled,
huddled in entranceways,
waiting to be shuttled
to the T,
its underground
rumble muddled
by the grumble
of beggars on the street,
heads bent.

"Ma'am! You,
with the kind face,
please." But I am masked
by this weather.
Gray. Changed.
I have become
the needy one,
unable to spare
even a word.

I wear no
face under
my umbrella,
melting my feet
in pools of
what once was
the sky.

Lub-Dub

Wound by the wind
to curl around a branch
like an apple peel
around a knife
and thus freed
from its original life
by the bramble's
own design, the leaf feels
it is possible to die
and still live on.

So taught by love
to rend and to evolve,
we revel in the wind,
in our own reversals,
revealing as we turn
the carnival colors
or our revolving,
reverberating hearts.

Mystery Hairs

They sprout overnight, curl impossibly
long from ankles and earlobes. Unruly
as unwashed dogs, they refuse to stand still,
to be smoothed into eyebrows, so willful
only the pluck of tweezers can stop
them.   I recall a set of clay men I shaped
when I was eight; lopsided, they toppled
in the car. Legs buckled, necks gaped
open, heads rolled on the floor. I refused
to take them in to school, that territory
of taunts and elbows.
                    This is a human story,
the forms we inhabit and the forms we choose,
flesh the mystery to which we're moored,
your shoulder in bed the slope of some wild shore.

Why I Had to Leave Town

A friend said to me,
speaking of my husband,
nearly thirty years my senior,
"Do you call him *Mr. Hart?*"
I was so angry, I couldn't answer.
Later I thought of a retort:
"Oh, you know, only in bed."
Another woman said to me,
"Do you have a good relationship
with your father?" I thought,
"Shut up! Go to hell!"
But my mouth said nothing.
At the grocery store, I paced
the aisles, still fuming.
When the bagger opened
his mouth to say, "Paper
or plastic?" I shouted,
"What do you care?
Shut up! Go to hell!"
I could tell by the haste
with which he packed my bags
it was time for me to go.

Anniversary Poem

A young couple drowned last summer
on Lake Erie, in the calm water
we could see from our honeymoon
window. For us a year's gone by like nothing,
but the future out in front of us, light and buoyant,
no longer seems certain as a destination.

Married just a year, their destination
was peace and quiet, a cabin and a summer
week alone. They rented a boat, the clear water
of the lake suggesting a second honeymoon
unmoored from everyday concerns. Nothing
weighing them down—the clouds buoyant

as spinnakers above them, their hearts buoyant—
they kissed their way to a new destination.
Time did not stop, but sailed faster. One summer
hour melted to three, him buoying her up in the water.
(We didn't get our feet wet on our honeymoon.
Friends asked us what we had seen. Nothing!

Each other!) When they looked up again, nothing
could be seen of the boat. Guideless and buoyant,
it had drifted away, seeking its own destination.
They had forgotten to anchor. Some mere
oversight. The husband swam for shore. What were
her choices? She swam after him, the honeymoon

over. (Meanwhile, we stayed in bed, honeymoon
sex a destination reached over and over, nothing
to slow us, our bodies rising together, buoyant,
first one on top, then the other, destination:
pleasure, every drop squeezed from a summer
afternoon.) They swam until they took on water,

until their arms and legs turned to water,
then weighted and sank. For three days, I mooned
in front of the television set, watched nothing
but the local station. The unnervingly buoyant
reporter said *presumed drowned* like *destination
of choice*. A double anniversary this summer:

our honeymoon, their deaths. Sun-swelled, buoyant,
summer days slip past us like bubbles underwater.
We're nothing if not destined to drift on.

The Lights Go Out in the Rented House on Christmas Eve

Wind sweeps around the corners of the house,
sounds and breaks—low moans of animals
reassuring each other. Leaves rustle
across the porch, shift, sticks of straw pulled close

for bedding. Your breath in the darkness
seems slight as an infant's against the full—
throated wind at the corners of the house.
Sounds break tonight. Low moans of animals

fill my head, and a subtle light throws
itself in stars and shadows on the quilt.
I smile a virgin's smile, slow, beautiful,
while our footprints sleep under a fresh snow
and wind sweeps clean the corners of our house.

Sonnet for an Ordinary Day

In-between meals, in the casual darkness
of a shared Coca-Cola, you could not
pass for a stranger, lover mysterious
as-seen-on-t.v. or those hot-to-trot
paperbacks they sell at the grocery.
No, you are more yourself than when we met,
your mismatched socks propped carelessly
on a chair, shirt unbuttoned, collar wet
from your just-washed hair. I know you as well
as I know a mouthful of soda pop
will fizz on my tongue. It's that wonderful
every time, expectation filled. Don't stop
filling me with your familiar love—pull
me to bed, let me drink up every drop!

Thief

If I could go back,
I would become
the pudgy, dark-haired
boy, and he would become
me. Yes, I would force him
to watch me flash
my get-away grin as I ran
with the rumpled
blossoms he had spent
days planting, their delicate
heads bunched in my fists,
my neon sneakers
smearing the dusky
petals into the sidewalk.

When I got home
to the boy's house,
his mother, also soft
and dark-haired,
would scoop me up
in a hug, inhaling
the musk of violets
that still clung
to my t-shirt, my fingers,
while back in my yard,
the boy walked slowly
over flower beds
robbed of that scent.

Poem for the Arguing Neighbors

We had a new argument, a fresh fight
every day. One by one they kept blooming
like the zinnias that opened up overnight.

We yelled till the red of our faces turned white.
It was easy to see what was looming:
we had a new argument, a fresh fight

that drew blood. It flowered, red and bright
on the linoleum as the scarlet consuming
the zinnias. They opened up overnight

while we slept, him curled in a tight
fist around me, his body always assuming.
We had a new argument, a fresh fight.

My mother saw me in the front porch light.
Do not go back, she said. She was fuming.
The zinnias had opened up overnight,

their petals blown back, their slight
eyes pulled wide, the yellow mushrooming.
We had a new argument, a fresh fight.
The zinnias had opened up overnight.

Leftovers

Your niece can't speak or touch the place that hurts
her. She moans and claws her IV's out until
even the Jell-O-bearing nurse grows curt:
"She needs restraints. We have to keep her still."

The hospital is strange without your mother,
who's home with cancer, can't go out in public
without a mask to shield her from what hovers
around us all. In the car, you rub your neck;

we've missed the exit. We do this every week.
I pull a box of chocolates from behind the seat:
just marshmallow, coconut, the bleak
leftovers. What the hell, we eat

them all, fake smiles, say, "See? We *can* cope,"
choking down our last morsels of hope.

Happy Birthday

I want to know where
they are, the dogwood
trees I knew
as a child, their
open white
blossoms as broad
as my palms.

I raise my arm
and spread
out my fingers
to demonstrate
the way the petals
radiated from the thin
brown branches.

"I don't think those exist,"
my husband says
and smiles. But they must—
they are that clear
in my mind,
or in my memory
of my mind

when I was a girl
with hands as small
as flower-heads,
with fingers white
as petals.

Woman at the Water's Edge
after a photograph

She stands, bare feet
on wet granite,
her back to the camera,
her face turned towards
the water, her arms
open to the sky.

She has found
a balance, a connection,
though she is not rock
or cloud or wave, but warm
flesh, her naked
shoulder showing the contour
of muscle, her fingers

weaving the breeze
that ruffles her hair,
the hem of her dress.

She could be dancing,
about to spin out
of the frame, singing
or shouting, or she
could be leaning
ever-so-slightly forward,
learning, as I am
at this moment,
the wonder of stillness,
of concentration,
the pleasure
of taking it all in.

Remnants

Even though a boy will leave his home,
a girl her family, part of a man
remains in the kitchen, his mother's hands
slim and slippery with suds, her nylons,
silky, seamed, beneath her ruffled apron.
With your mother gone, the flower-stand
propped against the stone, laughter (canned)
escaping from her ancient television,
you sort through letters, photographs, relive
fragments of her life through the flotsam
of her desk. I do small things that matter
now, clear the kitchen drawers, give
each knife, each spoon a lesson in reflection,
return the sink to a bright, familiar clatter.

The Middle of Life

Zinnias are quiet
in the middle of life.
Their edges only *look* sharp
in the dry air.

Again and again, petal
by petal, the soul
repeats itself!
There is a hush

at the center
that pulls the bees in.
Later, we will miss
this life inside of life.
Dying in the yard

is one life—warm faces
separate along a fence,
ungathered petals cool
under a tree. Short

and sweet as the light
is now, zinnias
with their long tongues,
drink from all directions.

Late Definitions

A neighbor is one who lives
or is situated near another—
a fellow human being.
To neighbor is to lie close to
or border on. In bed, our feet
are neighbors, two and two
alike, down at the foot of the bed.
Our hands are neighbors,
depending on how we lie,
one set of fingers crooked
in another, or palms pressed
together. Our lips can be neighbors
as well—this depends on the verb—
kissing or talking inches apart,
our heads resting on neighboring
swells of pillows. Here we meet
in ways that can only be described
as neighborly, our borders touching,
crossing over, moving together,
subtly and not so subtly redefined.

About the Author

Gwen Hart holds degrees from Wellesley College and Hollins University. Her poetry has appeared in various journals and anthologies including *The Formalist*, *Romantics Quarterly*, *Poems for a Beach House*, and *Stories from Where We Live: Great Lakes*. She and her husband Roger, author of the short story collection *Erratics*, are MFA students at Minnesota State University, where Gwen is the associate editor of *Mankato Poetry Review*. This is her frist book of poems.

The New Women's Voices Series:

No. 1   *Looking to the East with Western Eyes*
         by Leah Maines

No. 2   *Like the Air*
         by Joyce Sidman

No. 3   *Mama Thoughts*
         by Gayle Pierce

No. 4   *The Time It Takes*
         by Kathy Ackerman

No. 5   *Drawing Lessons*
         by Carol Barrett

No. 6   *Girl in Garden*
         by Sandra Graff

No. 7   *Flower Half Blown*
         by Cheryl Snell

No. 8   *Path of Fire*
         by Christa Polkinhorn

No. 9   *Losing Ohio*
         by Gwen Hart